MORE CLASSROOM CLANGERS

MORE
CLASSROOM
CLANGERS

Selected and Compiled by

John G. Muir

Illustrated by GEORGE J. GLASS

GORDON WRIGHT PUBLISHING
25 MAYFIELD ROAD, EDINBURGH EH9 2NQ
SCOTLAND

Reprinted 1987

British Library Cataloguing in Publication Data

More classroom clangers.
1. English wit and humor. 2. Education
—— Anecdotes, facetiae, satire, etc.
1. Muir, John G.
827'.914'080355   PN6231.E3/

ISBN 0-903065-54-1

Typeset by Gordon Wright Publishing Ltd.
Printed by Billing & Sons Ltd. Worcester.

Contents

To
Gwen, Valerie and Lesley.

Preface

The response to *Classroom Clangers* was overwhelming. Many wrote to say how much they had enjoyed the book and encouraged me to put together another selection. Others contacted me offering a host of howlers which they had remembered or had noted down from their teaching experience over many years. While I suspect that some are apocryphal and that others may have grown in the telling, if I had a good laugh I considered it worthwhile to add them to my own personal collection. I am sure that this selection of the best from the hundreds I have received will raise a few laughs around the country.

John G. Muir

Telling Tales

The teacher was rather puzzled when one of her pupils came to school regularly with a lot of biscuits which he distributed among his friends. She thought she would ask him where he got them, but he refused at first to tell her. Thinking that he may be up to some mischief she took him aside and insisted that he tell her. 'Please Miss, my mum works in the biscuit factory and she smuggles them out in her knickers...' he blurted out to the shocked teacher.

Having successfully quietened the group of children in the dining room, the headmaster folded his arms and calmly said, 'Now, you will all sit there and eat your lunch without opening your mouths.'

'Please Sir, what did you write at the foot of my page?' 'Can't you read boy, it says "your writing is illegible".'

From a secondary school handbook, an unfortunate example of the school's discipline referral system.
'When a pupil is referred by an assistant teacher for refusal to carry out a punishment exercise, that pupil should be warned by the Principal Teacher and suspended in that teacher's room for the rest of the day ...'

A youngster spilled milk on his trousers one morning and leapt to his feet shouting 'Good God, look what I've done!' The young teacher was horrified and sent him to the headmaster to report he had used bad language. He arrived at the headmaster's study, knocked quietly and was admitted. 'Please Sir, Miss Nichols has sent me here for using bad language.' 'Good God boy!' said the headmaster, 'What on earth did you say?'

The boys' school was to become co-educational after the holidays with a first influx of girl pupils. The lads were quite excited and one arrived home to report to his parents, 'Guess what? After the holidays the school's becoming bisexual.'

Noticeboard

Will staff please note that the large space at the front of the building is reserved for the Headmaster.

If you think you have a problem you should see the head teacher.

It is easy to electrocute yourself with this equipment. You must ask the teacher how to use it.

If you find any big drips in your classroom this morning please report them to the janitor.

The Keep Fit Club will be held in the gym at lunch time each Monday. Mr. Leadbetter is looking for another member of staff to support him.

Any chemicals in the lab. cupboard marked 'poison' must only be given to members of staff.

Dear Teacher

The unconscious clanger in a parent's letter is a constant source of amusement to teachers.

Please excuse Mary being absent from school as I had to go to bed and oblige,
Yours truly, Mrs. Watson.

Sir, My daughter never had beasts in her hair until she came to your school.

Billy is ill with swelling in his throat. The doctor says it's gathering of the clans.

I'm sorry Peggy is unable to attend school as she fell and cut her knee on a piece of glass and is now suffering from a pane in the leg.

I regret to say Walter is in bed with a chill again. I just can't get him to pass water. He insists on jumping into every puddle he sees.

Jimmy returned home yesterday extremely distressed after he vomited up the High Street.

Bobby was not able to come to school because he hasn't been yet. The doctor says that it would be better if he stayed at home until he goes. When he has gone I will send him back.

John has been given until the month of March to recover.

I am sorry George was absent from school yesterday, but he had the skitters. (Sorry I can't spell the proper word).

Sorry Jimmy is late this morning as he hurt his neck and I overslept into the bargain.

Sorry Eric was absent this morning as he was extremely sick after breakfast.
P.S. I am not a very good cook yet.

Dear Mr. Forbes, Thankyou for your letter. I am glad you admit you were wrong, which just goes to show that teachers aren't imflammable.

Pamela will take squash, she is willing to be couched on Mondays.

Pauline is late because she had toothache. I told her she would have to go to the dentist, but she seems to be alright now.

Please excuse Marion from stripping for P.E. as she has had a bit of a chill and is suffering from a touch of diarrhoea. Would it be alright if she did it in her tracksuit?

12

Jim could not come to school this morning as he spent most of the night vomiting up the shepherd's pie and trifle he had for his supper. I think he must have caught a virus.

I would like my son to have a real vacation like teaching.

Dear Teacher, I didn't send Peter to school yesterday as I was told you were on strike.
Yours sincerely, Mrs. Smith.
P.S. I have just heard that you did go on strike. If I had been told about this earlier, I would not have written this letter to apologise.

Tommy and his sister were absent from school as they were suffering from conjunctivitis. I kept them off for a couple of days to keep an eye on them.

Parent: Why is my daughter's mark for French so low?
Teacher: She has been a bit lazy recently so we thought we would give her a fright.
Parent: What are you running here, a French department or a blooming ghost train?

One of the unsatisfactory aspects of asking pupils to deliver letters to their parents is highlighted by this letter from a father dated June 1985.
'Last week my daughter opened her schoolbag and, with a look of total innocence, handed me a letter. It informed me that the school would be closed the following Thursday because of the Pope's visit to Bellahouston Park!' (This visit took place in 1982).

Please excuse Bobby for being late. We had a very big dinner today.

Michelle's new shoes has skint her heals and I couldn't get a pear on her feet. When they are well heeled I'll send her back.

A boy had been sent home with a note from the school nurse informing his parents that he had nits in his hair and that they should follow the instructions on the bottle of shampoo. Next day came a short reply: 'It is the school's job to put something into his head, not to tell others how to take things out!'

Lesley was absent yesterday because she had an upset tammy.

I don't care what you right on his report card I no he is not stubid.

Sorry my son was off school last week when you were doing the eye cue test.

William's skin trouble is not termites (dermatitis) as we first thought.

14

Minor Mistakes

A little lad, always anxious to pass on a tale about another pupil, approached the teacher's desk after the interval with, 'Charlie never done the toilet.' The teacher, more anxious about the grammar than the apparent misdemeanor replied, 'Now Tommy, is it "did", "done" or "went"?' 'Oh yes Miss, he went but he never done it.'

When Mummy is angry, she puts on a teacher's voice. She sort of talks like a lady.

Billy, age 5, said that he was going to his Granny's for his holidays. The teacher was a little concerned because the school break had not begun. How long will you be off, Billy?' After some deliberation he replied, 'I'm not sure Miss, but I'll tell you when I get back.'

The Head Teacher was showing two new infants around his school, chatting to them about the school rules and stressing how important it was for them to always do what the teachers told them. Suddenly he saw a pupil racing at full tilt along the corridor and shouted at the top of his voice, 'NEIL!!!' Instantly, the two youngsters at his side knelt down! He has been frightened of his power ever since.

John was very envious of the fact that his big brother, much older than he, was allowed out late at night to go to the cinema. In his 'News Book' he wrote: 'Colin gets to go to the pictures and is allowed up till he gets back.'

I didn't kick Peter first, I missed!

On his first day at school one little lad asked to go to the toilet. The infant teacher showed him where it was and returned to her room nearby. Presently the classroom door was pushed open by the same boy with his trousers round his ankles: 'Whose job is it about here to wipe bottoms?'

I know it is time to get up when I hear Mummy sharpening the toast.

When the teacher was listening to one of her pupils reading at her desk, the child said, 'Please Miss, you smell like my baby brother!' She was taken aback, then she realised that she too used baby powder. Next day it was back to a more delicate fragrance after her shower!

Did I see you writing on the wall, Peter?
No Sir, I was drawing!

Three answers from infants who were asked what we call a man who cuts down trees.
1. Peter's Dad.
2. A hatchet man.
3. A woodpecker.

'Tell me', said the Headmaster to the class of first infants, 'Can anyone in this room read yet?' There was a pause. 'Yes, the teacher, Sir.'

The little girl seemed delighted to announce that she knew for certain that her mother's age was either 34 or 36. 'How do you know, Elizabeth?' the teacher enquired. She giggled for a bit and then revealed that she had seen an item of her mother's underwear and had read her age on the label. After all, didn't all her own clothes have 'Age 5-7' on the back!

The teacher wasn't sure how to react when a seven year old in her class declared 'I wish I was Gay.' Before she could open her mouth to speak, he continued '... she's got a horse and lives on a farm.'

'Now Susan, what does this letter say?'
'Please Miss, I've never heard it say anything.'

Teacher to a farmer's son, 'What would your father do if he had a field that was flooded? (Hopefully awaiting 'drain it') 'Keep out of it, Miss.'

Why do we keep zoo animals in cages? To keep the people out, Miss.

The infant teacher had already dismissed her pupils after their first day at school and had seen them safely off the premises. She returned to her classroom to find one little girl sobbing in her seat. 'Whatever is the matter, Jenny?' she enquired, putting her arm around her. 'Mummy says I've to stay here until I'm sixteen.' was the worried reply.

When I grow up I'm going to marry a shriek with lots of money.

Mummy, I got a reading book today but it's not nearly as good as the one you read to me at night. This one keeps using the same words.

'It's 25th January... 'Whose birthday is it today?' asked the teacher who normally sang 'Happy Birthday' for any of the pupils whose birthday fell on a school day, but had hoped that someone would remember Scotland's national bard. There was a long pause. 'Haven't you heard of Robert Burns?' 'He's not in this class, Miss', a wee lad in the front quickly exclaimed.

The innocence of childhood can also have an effect on discipline, as the following story illustrates: The Headmaster was watching a group of infants, newly enrolled that morning, playing happily together. From the window he saw one of them suddenly begin to punch and kick another child. Anxious, not only to stop the fight but to assert his authority with a new pupil, he quickly went outside and marched the child towards his study. Swinging the door open ahead of the little boy he had no time to say anything before, in all innocence the lad said, looking up coyly, 'This is a nice house, who lives here?'

The teacher was discussing 'People who help us' and the subject at that moment was the doctor.
'What does the doctor do for you?'
'Gives you pills when you are sick, Miss.'
Like a shot, one little lad interjected, 'When I'm sick my Mummy runs for a bowl!'

The name of Roberson Cruso's friend was Good Friday.

Colin's new duffle coat had been put on the cloakroom floor, not on the pegs as he had been clearly instructed, so the teacher was rather annoyed when she was told about it. 'And you just walked over it ... ' 'No, Miss, I jumped over it', was the indignant reply.

The teacher was trying to explain the meaning of the expression 'He works twenty-four hours a day.' After some thought one lad retorted that his Dad worked twenty-five hours a day. Before the teacher could explain that this would be impossible, he continued, ' ... you see, he works during his dinner hour.'

18

From an infant 'News Book'; the saga starts two weeks before the birthday.

14 days to go: It is my birthday soon. I hope to get a horse.

12 days to go: Mummy says she likes horses too.

8 days to go: I can't wait to get a horse for my birthday.

3 days to go: Daddy says horses cost a lot of money.

2 days to go: I will call it Prince if it is a boy.

Birthday: I got a hamster for my birthday. It is called Goldy.

The day after: Mummy is scared of Goldy. Daddy helps me to hold it. I think Mummy would have liked a horse better.

The teacher was talking about famous people, pop stars, T.V. personalities etc. One little girl did not seem to be interested and appeared to be dreaming, so, as every good teacher is trained to do, she asked her a question to involve her. 'What would you like to do if you were a star, Susan?' Her quick and half-dazed reply was 'Twinkle, Miss!'

It was Christmas lunch at the little village school and the teacher gave a lecture on eating all the lovely food that had been prepared for them, particularly when boys and girls in many parts of the world were going hungry. The teacher ended with ' ... and it's chicken today!' As quick as a flash the gamekeeper's son piped up, 'Thank goodness, I'm fed up with pheasant.'

A teacher, supervising the dining hall noticed that a plate had been pushed into the centre of the table with the vegetables untouched. Six five year olds were sitting at the table and she asked them whose plate it was in an attempt to get the child to at least eat some. But she tried in vain as they all denied that it was their plate. However, an older girl, the sister of one of the children came over to ask what was wrong. One of the youngsters replied in a loud voice, 'I left my vegetables and the teacher wants to know who did it.'

The class was suddenly interrupted by a gigantic sneeze from a little girl at the back of the room. 'Susan, what do you say?' asked the teacher. 'Bless me, Miss', was the quick reply.

I am Jimmy.
I love my Mother.
I love my Father.
I love my Sister.
I love my Dog.
I love my Budgie.
But not all of them love me.

Teacher: 'Now boys and girls, you will have to be on your toes for this one.' At this, the children stood up.

The little boy excitedly announced to his teacher that his mummy had brought a baby boy back from the hospital. 'And what is his name?' asked the teacher. 'I think it's Spot', he replied. 'That's an interesting name', said the teacher, diplomatically. Later that day when Dad called at the school he said to the teacher, 'I suppose John has told you the news?' 'We're calling him Mark.'

I like bacon, but not when it's rusty.

The infant class were singing the children's song:
I've got a little light,
I'm going to let it shine,
Let it shine,
Let it shine,
Let it shine.
'The battery will run out', said one concerned little boy.

Every infant teacher used to reversals of letters when teaching will appreciate this one:
Teacher: 'What should you do when you discover fire?
Child: Dial P.P.P.

A primary class visited the local library. The teacher anxious to imbue an interest in reading told the class to pick any book.
Child clutching very heavy tome: 'Please Miss, who is this guy Harold Pinter?'
Teacher (slightly surprised): He is a very, very good writer.
Child (thinks for a moment and then): Does that mean he can do his 'W's?

We don't have sheets or blankets on our beds now. Mummy bought two lovely soft bidets.

'Doreen, has your mother got a washing machine?'
'She's got two, Miss. One that wets the clothes and one that drys them.'

Writing Wrongs

A solicitor is someone who breaks up your marriage and charges you for it.

Every American President shows his respect for his country. He stands up, swears, and salutes the stars and strips.

Another name for a 'public conveyance' is a toilet.

In a lesson on the comparison of adjectives, the teacher set the class some examples to work out, among them being 'ill'. One rather pessimistic pupil wrote, 'ill, worse, dead.'

'Please Miss, how do you spell "fought"?'
'Do you mean as in "two boys fought in the playground", Susan?'
'No, Miss, I mean the fought you fink in your head.'

A down bed is a bed on the floor.

Terra Cota is stuff squeezed out of little insects and used to turn puddings red.

What is dusk? Little bits of fluff that fly about in the air.

An epigram is something you send if you are in a hurry.

Her mother, being immortal, died.

The old man kept lots of ancient things in his house. He was specially interested in old bras. Round the fireplace he had nailed lots of old bras of different shapes and sizes taken from his farm horses.

A rhetorical question is a question you know there is no answer to like, 'What has the government been doing since it came into power?'

A sure-footed animal is one which does not miss when it kicks you.

He was very ill and lost his conscience.

Irrigation is when the farmer wets the field himself.

Another name for a bird watcher is a naturist.

The lady was very poor. When her husband died she asked the welfare to arrange a state funeral for him.

A catalogue is a dialogue for two people.

When the writer spoke of a 'hire car' he probably wanted one that gave him a better view.

Define the first person. Adam.

My father is a civil serpent.

All the teachers in our school are certified.

Inflation in the country is caused by . . .? A lot of hot air, Sir.

A good friend says nasty things to your face, not behind your back.

'Lingerie' means hanging about.

There is no doubt that people on television are uncovered in the most unexpected places so it is really worth the cost of the licence fee.

The Victoria Cross is a woman given to soldiers if they are good.

I stood on the cliff, the sea was rough and the wind roared and not a sole was to be seen.

Chivalry is when you feel cold.

It was a nice house, but the drains were unfit for human habitation.

The son came shinning in at the window.

A prospectus is a man who finds gold.

It was moonlight and the air was soft and putrid.

Nets are holes surrounded by pieces of string.

He had no difficulty getting out as he knew the building like the back of his head.

A period is a dot at the end of a sentence. A period costume is therefore one covered in dots.

Cereals are stories that go on and on.

An obituary is a home for lady dogs.

'Civility' means when you get out of the army.

Gender tells you when a man is masculine, feminine or neuter.

Punks who die and make their hair a funny colour are an eyesore.

The tyres were solid in those days and really hurt you when you went out and got cobbled.

Speedway riders must have nerves of steel, otherwise they would get killed, which is my ambition in life.

I always do half my homework on Friday night, half on Saturday night and the other half on Sunday night.

An anenome is a person who fights against you.

A tantrum is a kind of two seater bicycle.

A spectre is a man who goes to football matches.

If you didn't go to school you wouldn't learn good.

A martyr is someone who suffers for his or her briefs.

The people who lived in the country came into the town for special services such as hairdressing, banking and soliciting.

After being in the Brownies for some time you are publicly unrolled.

The expression used is 'Don't upset the apple tart' (apple cart).

Punctuality is hard to remedy once it is firmly established in the system.

Necessity is the mother of convention.

Today many people are in jail for committing suicide while under the influence of drink.

Seafaring men in the habit of drinking are liable to collide with other vessels.

What is a mediator? A man who says, 'Punch me instead.'

If a man takes alcohol, his wife and children suffer, and *vice versa*.

A surname is the name of a person you say 'Sir' to.

Everyone needs a holiday from one year's end to another.

Explain 'mortgage'. When people do not wish to have their deceased relatives buried, they send them to a mortuary to have their remains mortgaged.

'The lark that soars on dewy wing' means that the lark was going so high and flapping its wings so hard that it broke into perspiration.

Virgil was in love with a girl called Enid and wrote a lot of books about her.

A conjunction is a place where two railway lines meet.

The poem of the Forsaken Merman made me very angry, to think a woman could leave a poor helpless man to get his own meals.

Plato was the God of the Underground.

Do you think Shylock was necessarily a bad character? No, because after all, he had his living to make.

Write a sentence showing clearly the meaning of 'posterity'. The cat leaped about and then sat on its posterity.

A fort is a place to put men in, a fortress is a place to put women in.

In the eighteenth century travelling was very romantic, most of the high roads were only bridal paths.

Sailors do not like the sea when it is rough because it is very dangerous and many lives are lost and few of them found again.

Our seamen are cheerful, happy and brave, for they know nothing of things going to happen to them in the future.

The dodo is a bird that is nearly decent now.

George Bernard Shaw was a famous actor and comedian.

What do you know about Keats? I don't even know what a Keat is.

If it says 'anon' at the end of a poem it generally means that the author did not know who wrote it.

Shakespeare probably wrote Henry IV in two parts to leave room for the commercials.

A magnet is a thing you find in a bad apple.

A cynic is a man who refuses to believe in fairy tales.

A talisman is a man who calls every week for the furniture money.

A parsimonious boy is a boy who wants to be a parson.

Many new faces toed the line at the school marathon.

A philosopher is a man who makes the best of a bad job. Socrates is called a philosopher because he didn't worry much when he was poisoned.

A hostage is a big bird that buries its head in the sand.

A leper is a fierce wild animal.

Our food was eaten and our water was drunken.

It was simply a pigment of his imagination.

A skeleton is a man with his inside out and his outside off.

Man is the only animal who can strike a light.

The different kinds of senses are commonsense and nonsense.

A blood vessel is a man's lifeboat.

The home of the swallow is the stomach.

A fissure is a man who catches fish.

You cannot tell the gender of 'egg' until it is hatched.

The Press today is the mouth-organ of the people.

I searched for the missing book in every room and in each case the search was fatal.

A phlegmatic person is one who has chronic bronchitis.

Polonius was a mythical sausage.

Barely Biblical

What is the outward and visible sign or form in the rite of baptism? The baby.

A graven image was what was put in the ground over the bodies of dead people.

What is meant by the verse in the Bible, 'Sufficient unto the day is the evil thereof . . .', It means that you mustn't do too many bad things in the one day.

A parable was a heavenly story with no earthly meaning.

Insects smoked in the church where the worshippers gathered.

In these days you were not allowed to work in a week which had a Sunday in it.

I saw the Archbishop at my confirmation service and now I know what a crook looks like.

It seems the Parable of the Sower can be confusing to some: . . . and some seed fell on stony ground and the fowls of the air sprang up and choked them.

Who built the Ark? Joan.

The spies said that the Promised Land was a land 'flowing with milk and honey' and they brought back a bunch of grapes to prove it.

'Mummy, I heard that Jesus' father painted cars'. 'No dear, he was a joiner. What made you think that?' 'Well, the teacher said he was a car painter.'

Joseph lived a very straight life so Pharaoh made him a great ruler.

The man fell by the roadside but everyone walked past him except the good Sam Marathon.

The class had been told the story of Abraham and Isaac, emphasising that God was testing Abraham's faith when he commanded him to sacrifice his son on the altar. Asked later to write about the dramatic incident using their own words, one fellow wrote, '. . . there was I, bound hand and foot, stretched out on the altar. My father had a big knife in his hand and held it over me ready to plunge it into my stomach, when a big voice said, 'Abraham! Stop! You've passed your test.'

Alias was a good man mentioned in the Bible.

In a prize essay competition sponsored by the local church a child was writing about the story of Samuel on the subject 'How God talks to us.' Samuel's mother Hannah is speaking: 'If you give me a son, God, I'll give him back to you.' God replies: 'O.K. Hannah, it's a deal.'

Hymns and psalms are favourites for misquotation:

'He's got your wee brother in his hands'
(He's got you and me brother in his hands).

'In past George Green he leadeth me'
(In pastures green he leadeth me).

'We can sing though full we be'
(Weak and sinful though we be).

'A wean in a manger'
(Away in a manger).

The school chaplain was talking to a group of infants about 'peace'.
'Who was the greatest peacemaker?', he asked.
'Jesus', said a little girl.
'Yes, good, why?
'Well, he made 5000 'pieces' for the crowd of people who were hungry.'

Faith. That quality which enables us to believe that which we know to be untrue.

The teacher was a little confused when the little girl insisted that Mary and Joseph must have been freezing cold with no clothes on in the stable. The matter was cleared up when she read the line of the carol she had been teaching. 'Mary and Joseph in stable bare ... '

The infant teacher was amused when a little girl in her class said that the ark landed on Mount Anorak.

The infant class was asked to draw a picture of Mary and Joseph with the baby Jesus in the flight into Egypt. One little boy had a super drawing and the delightful finishing touch was a little suitcase on the donkey's back with 'J.C.' on it.

Birds and Bees

The pancreas is the gland that gives you sexual desire.

When a young girl reaches puberty she starts to have a monthly period and develops breasts, but fortunately these only last for five or six days.

My grandad was in the war and shot several times. He had to have an operation to take the bullets out. I think my mother was born just about this time.

When you want to make a baby you need a sperm from the father and an egg from the mother, but it is not always easy to get them together at the right time of the year.

The following examples were sent in to Grampian Television in response to their request for children's work after discussion of the programme 'Living and Growing'.

When you are small you don't need to worry about all these things, like sex etc.

A lot of people find sex something to laugh at but there is nothing funny about it. I bet even our parents found it funny when they were at school.

If nobody wanted babies there would be nobody left in the world.

When I saw the programme I was taught the most unlikely things.

The programme told us that every lady has a volvo.

I thought the programme was quite educational because if you met someone and you did not know what to do, you could always refer to the programme.

Every month a woman lets off an egg.

The programme explained how an egg is released from the ovary and does a twenty-eight day cycle along the Fallopian tube.

The sixth programme was about having the baby with names like labourer because it was hard work and looked it too.

Labour can start at any time. It is advisable to have a bag ready.

When the woman is nearly ready to give birth she starts to get contraptions.

. . . then they cut the biblical cord.

Next the midwife will take the baby in her arms and juggle the baby.

Hardly Historical

The crown was not passed on in his family because the king had no hair.

In 1918 there was a war and every year since we have had two minutes peace.

The South Sea Bubble was a scream for lending money to the government.

The low wages paid by the farmers led to the pheasants' revolt.

The ancient Britons used to fish in cockles and used to paint their faces so that they would know one another if they were drowned.

William the Conqueror was thrown from his horse and wounded in the Feudal System.

The Minister of War was a clergyman who preached to the soldiers in their barracks.

Simon de Montford formed what was known as the 'Mad Parliament'. It is something the same as we have at the present time.

William the Conqueror surrounded the Isle of Ely with his feet.

A crow at the mast-head of a French ship fired twice at Nelson and killed him.

Why does true English history begin with the reign of Henry VIII? Because up to this time it was all lies.

Guerilla warfare means up to their monkey tricks.

The budget is a list of grievances secretly presented to the Prime Minister to rectify the unemployed.

'Who said, "Kiss me Hardy"'? 'Laurel, Sir?'

In the Middle Ages the monks went into other peoples houses and helped everybody, doing every man's work. About this time the population of England increased threefold.

He was given the crown of Scotland and a stone scone.

They called them 'The Dark Ages' because it was before electric light.

Joan of Arc was Noah's sister.

The Duke of Monmouth was found lying in a ditch, with some peas in his pocket which he had eaten.

At the Battle of Crecy the soldiers found a motor car (ford) which they used to cross the river.

Sir Winston Churchill was the first Prime Minister to use an iron curtain.

The Russian Revolution started when the people rose up against the tar.

Hitler said that he wanted to have a larger living room for his people.

Hitler and his wife were found dead in a coal bunker at the end of the war. They had just got married and he did not want to surrender.

The last shots of the First World War were fired in a railway carriage. We celebrate it with Armistice Day each year.

During the war silk was very scarce because it was all used for par-shots.

The teacher told the class how, when General Wolfe stormed the Heights of Quebec, the soldiers rowed up the river in boats with muffled oars. One boy recorded this in his note book as 'the soldiers crept up the river with buffalos.'

Oliver Cromwell's nose was very large and a deep red colour but underneath it he was a very religious soul.

The Declaration of Indulgence in James's reign was when people were allowed to worship God in their own way. Seven bishops refused to do so and they were put on trial. They were found not guilty.

King Richard led the Crusaders to the Holy Land to fight against the Saccherins.

If the Premier dies, who officiates? An undertaker.

Where was the Magna Carta signed? At the bottom.

Napoleon lost his navel at the Battle of Waterloo.

With the Feudal System you had to lend each other your tractor.

Queen Elizabeth was pale and thin but she was a stout Protestant.

The greatest thing about Oliver Cromwell was the wart on his nose.

The first Roman sent to Britain was very cross with the people for not being christians.

Edward III would have been King of France if his mother had been a man.

Prisons in the Norman period were not like ours today. They were dull and dreary.

Boadicea was a brave woman. She fought herself and drove a chariot.

Robert the Bruce was a very brave leader who fought like a spider.

The Normans put moles around their castles to protect them from attack.

Where are the descendants of the ancient Britons to be found today? The British Museum.

Where were the Kings of Britain generally crowned? On their heads.

The King was crowned in the Crystal Palace with his sepulchre in his hand.

What do you know about Marconi? Marconi is used to make delicious puddings.

During the Great Fire of London, the worst flaming place of all was St Paul's Cathedral.

Lenin was the first revolting leader of Russia.

Why was he called 'God's silly vassal?' I don't know, it seems a silly name to call anybody.

Why did the industrial revolution start? Someone shot the Tsar.

The first women allowed to vote were called the Suffer Jets.

If John Knox were alive today he would turn in his grave.

The Poll Tax was to be paid by everyone with a head.

Where in the World?

Hush puppies pull sledges for Eskimos.

What do the French call the English Channel? It is a kind of perfume.

The sea in Denmark is called the scatty cat (Kattegat).

The Stock Exchange is a place in London where cattle and pigs are bought.

The horizon is a line where the earth and the sky meet, but disappear when you get there.

One of the chief dam places in Egypt is Aswan.

Eskimos hunt seals with large hairpins.

What is meant by the 'Relief of the Land'? If you have been out at sea on a boat and had a rough time, you would say that it is a relief to be back on the land again.

Marseilles is a large town on Frances bottom.

The hills between Scotland and England are called the Cheesies.

A place where towns and cities and lots of people live is called a conor basin.

In the north of Scotland some of the people speak Garlic.

A Fakir is a Hindu twister.

People who live in Italy are called Stallions.

Latitude tells you how cold you are and longtitude how hot you are.

China is called China because the first china was made there.

Take Ireland, the country where, if it isn't raining bullets on the politicians, it's raining water on the bogs.

The probable cause of earthquakes may be attributed to bad drainage and neglect of the sewage.

Name the English lakes. Ulleswater, Derwent Water and Bayswater.

The chief bays in the South of England are Torbay, Poole Bay and Bombay.

The inhabitants of Moscow are called Mosquitoes.

A cyclone is a man who rides a bicycle.

What are the main feeders of the Amazon? Alligators.

The meridian of Greenwich is a line that isn't there, kept at Greenwich to measure the time with.

Lemons are a quirk of nature. They commit suicide by jumping over cliffs into the sea.

Brussels is famous for its carpets and sprouts.

The Laplander lives by hunting and fishing. If he catches a whale he takes it home to his tent and his wife will cook it for his supper.

In Egypt they use large dames to store their water.

In India rats eat 20% of the rice crop. In Brazil they drink 20% of the coffee.

Clearly a budding Scottish Nationalist, one pupil asked to point out where England was on the map said, 'There, Miss, hanging on to the foot of Scotland.'

Sums and Segments

Air is made up of oxygen and sanatogen.

CO_2 is used for keeping people from dyeing and distinguishing fires.

Protractors are used for digging up potatoes.

A line is a length of breadth.

A curve is the longest way between two points.

To fill an apparatus with acidulated water, turn on the taps and acidulate.

What does nitric acid do? It burns yellow holes in your clothes.

How do nuclear scientists avoid the effects of radiation? They sit well back from the fire.

Oxygen has eight sides.

The triangle shown is all right.

A thermometer is for measuring how much water there is in milk, a hydrometer for measuring how much milk there is in water.

Gravity was discovered by Isaac Walton. It is chiefly noticeable in the autumn, when the apples are falling off the trees.

The Zodiac is the zoo in the sky where lions, goats, virgins and other animals go after they are dead.

To germinate is to become a naturalised German.

A circle is a round line with no kinks in it, joined up so as not to show where it began.

Chlorine gas is very injurious to the human body, and the following experiments should only be performed by the teacher.

Michael Holiday invented electricity.

An alkali is a chemical substance without water in it, like whisky.

What are nitrates? They are cheaper than dayrates.

The difference between 'mass' and 'weight' is that when you buy a sack of potatoes that is 'mass'. 'Weight' is when you carry it home.

The animal which has the greatest attachment to man is woman.

It is wise to get intoxicated before you go abroad to keep away strange diseases.

A vacuum is just another name for a Hoover.

Trees that stay green all year round are called artificial.

After an experiment during a science lesson, the teacher asked the class to write in their jotters what they had discovered. One child wrote, 'We discovered it was all very difficult.'

Newton discovered that when an apple becomes over ripe it falls to the ground.

In a country school the teacher always tried to relate the work to the general knowledge of the children. The gamekeeper's son was having difficulty with simple multiplication. 'If a salmon weighed five kilos and it was sold at 10p a kilo, what would it be worth? asked the teacher. 'It wouldn't be worth buying at that price!' came the informed reply, 'Unless it had been poached.'

Charles weighs 6 stone 12 inches.

'Come out all the mental people,' said the teacher to the arithmetic class.

Horse-power is the distance one horse can carry a pound of water in an hour.

A centimetre is an insect with a hundred legs.

Germs are small insecks that swim inside you when they can get in. Some are called measles, but you can't see them.

Anaemia is not having enough blood, but you have enough to bleed as much as anyone else if you cut your finger.

The Chiltern Hundreds are the things you see in cheese through a microscope.

Faintly Franglais

Je reçus à son adresse un coup d'épee dans la poitrine.
I received in his house a letter in poetry.

Montrez moi le chemin qui conduit à la ville.
Show me the shirts that were made in the town.

J'ai beau me défendre.
I have a gentleman to protect me.

C'est égal. Dès qu'ils furent loin, je sortie de ma cachette.
All the same, as furious as a lion, I took out my hatchet.

Oublier les glaces de son age.
Because of his age he was obliged to wear glasses.

Une grande foule attirée par les spectacles.
A crowd of people wearing spectacles.

Parchemin. A side road.

Heureusement, il est parti.
It was a hilarious party.

Il est d*éfendu de fumer.*
He is trying to defend his smoking.

Dépêchez-vous.
Would you like some peaches?

Qui habitaient la grande maison blanche?
Who whitewashed the big house?

Il portait une grande bague à la main gauche.
He was carrying a huge bag in his left hand.

Histoire de s'amuser. History made him laugh.

Je suis très heureux de faire votre connaissance.
I am very pleased to be connected with you.

Un filet mince de fumée.
A fillet of smoked mince.

C'est bon à travailler, mais ce n'est pas bon de pas le faire.
It is good to travel, but not so good to pay the fare.

The money was left in his will.
L'argent fut gauché dans sa volonté

I had to fly for my life.
J'avais à mouché pour ma vie.

Au bord de la mer. Aboard with mother.

Cela va sans dire. He walks without talking.

47

Plus ça change, plus c'est la même chose!
The more change you have the more difficult it is to chose.

Défense d'afficher. No fishing!

Mal de mer. Mother is ill.

Mes memoirs sont peu précis. My memoirs are precious few.

Un homme d'esprit. A publican.

Gros fils de vierge. Large sons of the virgin.

Avoirdupois. Have some green peas.

Food for Thought

If you cannot find an onion, take a leak instead.

'Baking blind' means putting something in the oven and not bothering to look at it.

Another way of doing potatoes is to do them with your jacket on.

Liver and kidney are awful (offal).

Egg whites make a souffle blow up. Gelignite makes it set.

Pastas come from Cornwall.

Apple grumble is my favourite pudding.

If you do not take enough vitamin C you will most likely suffer from vitamin D.

The Domestic Science teacher, trying to teach her pupils economy: 'Don't waste the apples, they don't grow on trees you know!'

Bass is a beverage made from the fish of the same name.

You'll sleep better if you drink desecated coffee before bedtime.

Why does the grocer sell cured ham? Because he couldn't sell it if it was still ill.

Caviare generally comes from a surgeon.

Experiments have shown that vitamin E makes rats sexy. We don't know about men yet.

To work best in a kitchen, especially in a hotel, it is important for a woman to be absolutely sterile.

Oysters are usually found in beds at the seaside.

What is the best known cereal in Britain? Coronation Street.

In Italy they are very fond of food such as graffitti.

'A la carte' means you can have everything that's on the trolley.

When fresh vegetables are not available you can always go and get canned.

If you can eat it it is eligible.

Please Miss, I couldn't spell scones so I've put buns instead.

The mixture in the bowel will make nine buns.

Carbohydrates are fattening. Carbolodrates are not.

A nice finishing touch is to top the cake with camel icing.

Hold the prawn between your fingertips. Straighten it out, then jerk its head and bottom together. The prawn will immediately jump out of its jacket.

If baking powder is not added to the plain flour your scones will not stand and may end up as pancakes.

Gently knead the dough until it is round and flat adding a sprinkle more flour if knead be.

The wine is best chilled and served in a giraffe.

Salt is stuff which, if it is not boiled with potatoes, makes them nasty.

Why not eat Italians for a change. Spaghetty bolagnaged and a glass of good red wine make a nice change.

Mostly Musical

Archipelagos are the high runs in music which only the best people can sing.

An interval in music is a period for refreshment.

An octet is a figure with eight sides.

D.C. means don't clap!

I like the song we learned, I think it was a Negro spiritual, 'Take me back to old Virginity'.

How long do you hold a minim for? Three seconds?

A theme is the thing that runs down the leg of your trousers.

A pibroch is a Scotsman with wind.

Cabarets are entertainments where they can't afford a stage.

The smallest members of the percussion family are tangerines.

A crotchet is a table cloth with fancy sewing.

What do you do when you find a note with a dot after it? Stop.

What does legato mean? With a limp.

What do we find below a mezzo-soprano? A stool.

Why do you think the composer wrote the work in two flats?
He probably stayed with friends at times.

Inspectors at Large

An inspector was sent to a small rural school following a complaint from parents that the teacher there was spending an inordinate amount of time on religious studies. On knocking and entering the classroom he found the teacher and the children all on their knees praying. But the teacher was equal to the occasion. 'Arise, children', she said, 'our prayers have been answered.'

An inspector has a fund of stories about visits to country schools. One such story concerned his arrival at a small rural school one forenoon. It was playtime, and as he made for the entrance he was confronted by a small boy who barred his way and said:

'Did you brush your shoes this morning?'
'Yes, I did.'
'Did you wash your face?'
'Yes, I did that too.'
'And did you remember to brush your teeth?'
'Yes, I gave them a good brush.'
'It's just as well', said the boy. 'The Inspector's coming today.'

On a tour of schools on a remote Scottish island, an Inspector arranged his programme so that the tiny, one-teacher school close to his base was left until last. He arrived there on the Friday morning to a rather chilly reception.
'All week we have watched you driving past our door', said the teacher, 'and the children have been so disappointed.' 'And do you know', she continued, 'these poor girls have had clean white socks on every morning!'

When an inspector from the city visited a small country school he described his home town as a place where everything was dull and grimy, there were few birds, there was a lot of smoke and all you could see were chimneys and roof-tops. 'What sort of place do I come from, do you think?' 'Sounds like a prison, sir.'

Every teacher knows that effective follow-up work is essential after an outdoor study; it is often the part which many children least like if it is not done well. This is illustrated by a conversation overheard by an inspector who quietly joined on to the end of a snake of children making their way back to school along the edge of a playing field. 'Look Billy, there's a rabbit!' 'For goodness sake, don't tell the teacher John, or she'll have us writing about it, or drawing it.'

An Inspector was visiting a school in a deprived district of a town where the kids were a really rough bunch. He decided to start his inspection with a few questions on mental arithmetic and addressed the first one to a boy in the front row. 'Can you tell me what is seven times eight?' The boy immediately responded with 'fifty-six'. 'Not bad', said the Inspector. 'Not bad?', said the boy, 'What do you mean, it's perfect!'

Arty Crafty

After the woodwork teacher had stressed to the class that the glue should be spread thinly on the joint, he asked a boy who appeared to be half asleep, 'What, Smith, should you *not* do with the glue?' The boy's answer was a sign of the times. 'Sniff it, Sir.'

The art teacher thought he had explained the meaning of 'tone' and 'shade', until one boy wrote that 'tone' is a colour and 'shade' is using an H.B. pencil.

Please Sir, can I do one colour over another because I want to do the girl's hair dyed?' 'Why not just paint the colour you want it to be?' 'Please Sir, because this might be the first time anybody's ever done a picture of dyed hair.'

My father is an artist but he only draws the dole just now.

Michael Angelo painted the cistern of the chapel.

Asked what he knew about the Impressionist Period, one pupil replied that it was a time when paintings made a great impression on people.

Art Teacher: Yes, the face is very good Norman, you seem to have mastered the idea of shading the nose. I'll just paint out that mark on the lip for you and it will be fine.
Pupil: No, no, Sir, leave it! It's supposed to be a bogie.

What forced the actor to return to the theatre?
The roar of the greasepaint, the smell of the crowd.

On a report card from a woodwork teacher:

All the other boys have produced coffee tables or lamp standards, but alas, Jeremy has only been able to produce a small brown stool.

Afterflaws

Looking for the word 'wedge', the teacher asked the class, 'what small thing could I use to keep the door open? The amusing response from one pupil was 'You could get a wee boy from the infant room.'

What did the man mean when he said 'Time will tell'? He meant that he would phone the speaking clock.

An amoeba is a small orgasm you usually get in water.

When he says 'he executed his business there', it is just another way of saying he gave it the chop.

If all education were abolished in the world today the effects would be felt in the world to come.

An autobiography is a book about cars.

Things bundled together are called a cloister.

Explain the meaning of 'What he said was sharp and to the point.' It means that he was very blunt when he spoke.

Daddy hasn't managed to give up smoking completely, but he has cut it down by a hundred per cent.

The teacher explained that graminivorous meant eating grass and carnivorous meant eating flesh. 'What would you call an animal that eats everything?' he asked. 'A greedy glutton' was the apt response.

Bona fide: Well fed.
            Good dog.

At the Coronation they could not use the Queen for practising so they used a real lady instead.

When pheasants are sold you have to buy them in braces.

A pupil was asked to stand up and give a sentence with the word 'canal' in it. He offered 'At 3.30pm when the bell goes we canal go home.'

Three shots rang out. Two men fell dead and the other went through his hat.

A teacher was wearing a badge 'Teachers for Peace' which depicts a dove and a book. A little girl was fascinated by the badge.
'What's the badge for, Miss?
'What do you think it means?
'When you want peace, you give us a book?'

Complete the following Susan: 'It takes two to make ... '
(Looking for the answer 'a quarrel')
'Love', was the coy suggestion.

James Joyce is famous for his book *All Sizes*.

An avenue is really just another name for a road but there are no council houses on them.

What is a dictator? My sister has one in her office.

In 1956 the Swedish Education Minister said that sex was compulsory for all school children.

Anxious that the boys should behave themselves when they went to their grandparents for a short stay, they were coaxed to be on their best behaviour. However, the young one said, 'What will we get if we are good?' The older boy was quite shocked. 'That's terrible Michael, you should be like me and be good for nothing.'

It is very important in Britain to show your birth certificate to prove that you have been born.

A minister's stipend is what he preaches his sermons on.

Jesus helped leopards to get rid of their spots.

The man asked Jesus what he could do to inherit internal life.

The class teacher was very concerned about one little boy in her room whose personal hygiene left a lot to be desired, so she wrote a very tactful letter to the mother suggesting that regular baths might solve the problem. Back came the reply: Dear Teacher, There is no problem. It is your job to teach, not to smell!

'We have three cats and one is a tom, but we are getting him dressed', explained the child to the teacher. 'Fancy putting clothes on a cat', a voice exclaimed from the back of the room.

Who wrote the Bible? Wm. Collins & Sons Ltd.

Baby sheep are called ... ?
Baby sheep are called in winter.

The bride carried a bunch of flowers on her weeding day.

Prices tend to flatuate quite often.

'Untapped potential' means being able to have a telephone conversation without anyone listening in.

Correct the following: a) The hen has three legs. b) Who done it? One small boy seeing some connection between the two answered: 'The hen never done it, God done it.'

Moths don't eat much. They just eat holes.

When you stroke a cat by drawing your hand along its back, it cocks up its tail like a ruler so you can't get any further.

61

Teachers' Talk

Communicates fluently: A constant chatterbox.

An independent learner: Will not do what he is told.

Mixes well with other pupils: Always chasing the girls.

Could try harder: A lazy little rascal.

Will go far: An absolute con man.

A born leader: A real little bossy boots.

Enjoys physical education: That's about all he can do.

Is good with his hands: He still can't read a word.

He cannot wait to leave school: ... and neither can we!

An active class member: Will not sit still for two minutes.

Has a facility with numbers: Will probably excel at bingo.

Exams have never been a problem with him: Has never turned up for one yet.

Has a ready ear for music: Never takes off his personal stereo.

A colourful personality: Her hair is dyed illuminous green.

His artwork has been displayed in every corridor: We have now confiscated the aerosol.

Has easily mastered a second language: Swears like a trooper.

His work will no doubt improve next year: It's a pity he leaves school this summer.